SUMMARY of PRIDE & PREJUDICE

A FastReads Summary with Key Takeaways & Analysis

NOTE: The purpose of this FastReads summary is to help you decide if it's worth the time, money and effort reading the original book (if you haven't already). FastReads has pulled out the essence with commentary and critique—but only to help you ascertain the value of the book for yourself. This summary is meant to be a supplement to, and not a replacement for the original book.

Copyright © 2017 by FastReads. All rights reserved. This book or parts thereof may not be reproduced in any form, stored in any retrieval system, or transmitted in any form by any means—electronic, mechanical, photocopy, recording, or otherwise—without prior written permission of the publisher, except as provided by United States of America copyright law. This is an unofficial summary. This is an unofficial summary for educational purposes and is not intended as a substitute or replacement for *Pride and Prejudice*.

TABLE OF CONTENTS

PLOT SUMMARY..4

CHAPTER SUMMARIES 5

ABOUT THE AUTHOR..31

MAJOR CHARACTERS 32

THEMES...35

ANALYSIS..37

PLOT SUMMARY

When the wealthy and single Bingley rents a manor in town, all the Bennets can think of is marriage and good fortune for their five daughters. Bingley takes to Jane, the eldest of the Bennet daughters, and Darcy, his friend, comes off as too proud to get along with anyone. He won't dance with Elizabeth, the second-eldest of the Bennet daughters and the protagonist, but she doesn't like him anyway, so no harm done.

Collins, the newly-appointed clergyman and cousin to Mr. Bennet, asks to marry Elizabeth to keep the Bennet estate, which is going to be his inheritance, in the family. Elizabeth won't marry such an unreasonable and self-deceptive man. Instead, she takes to Wickham, who is one of the officers new in town, and who claims that Darcy cheated him out of his inheritance.

Meanwhile, Darcy, who has been spending considerable time in the company of Elizabeth, is falling for her. He proposes to Elizabeth, but she won't marry him if he were the last man on earth. She says as much. He writes her a letter to explain his sour relationship with Wickham and to own up to the role he played in breaking up Jane and Bingley. He wins her over when he demonstrates a considerable change of character and convinces Wickham, who had eloped with Lydia (another of Elizabeth's sisters), to do the honorable thing and marry the otherwise ruined girl.

Bingley returns to town, woos the depressed Jane, and proposes to her. Darcy's wealthy aunt tells Elizabeth that Darcy won't marry a woman without a respectable family or connections and threatens her with censure and disregard. Elizabeth, tenacious as ever, stands up to her and accepts Darcy's proposal. Mrs. Bennet is over herself with joy; three of her daughters are finally married.

CHAPTER SUMMARIES

CHAPTER 1

"It is a truth universally acknowledged, that a single man in possession of a good fortune, must be in want of a wife."

Mr. Bennet learns from his wife that a wealthy young man from north of England has rented the manor at Netherfield Park. Mrs. Bennet informs her husband that the young man, who goes by the name Bingley, is single and may likely fall in love and marry one of their five daughters. She urges her husband to visit him for the sake of their daughters, but Mr. Bennet demurs. He promises to send a good word for their second daughter Elizabeth, who, in his opinion, is not as ignorant or as silly as their other daughters. Mrs. Bennet protests that Elizabeth is neither as beautiful as Jane nor as good-humored as Lydia.

CHAPTER 2

Mr. Bennet pays a secret visit to Mr. Bingley and informs his wife about it the evening after. Mrs. Bennet is considering introducing the girls to Mr. Bingley at Elizabeth's upcoming ball when Mr. Bennet delivers the news, much to the astonishment of the ladies. Mrs. Bennet praises her husband for heeding her advice and looking out for the girls.

CHAPTER 3

Mrs. Bennet and her five daughters coerce Mr. Bennet to divulge more about Mr. Bingley's looks and character, but Mr. Bennet evades their questions. The ladies learn from their neighbor, Lady Lucas, that Bingley is handsome and agreeable and intends to attend the next assembly at Meryton.

A few days later, Mr. Bingley returns Mr. Bennet's visit. He anticipates meeting the five ladies whose beauty he has heard of, but he only meets Mr. Bennet in his library. He discloses that he has to be in town the following day and so can't stay for dinner.

Mr. Bingley attends the assembly party with two of his five sisters, his brother-in-law Mr. Hurst, and his friend Mr. Darcy. The tall and handsome Darcy becomes the talk of the room when the guests learn that he makes ten thousand pounds a year.

However, he comes off as proud and condescending when he refuses to participate in the conversations and dancing. Mr. Bingley dances once with Elizabeth and twice with Jane, the eldest of the Bennet daughters. He is so captivated by the ball that he promises to give one at Netherfield Park. When Bingley nudges Darcy to dance with Elizabeth, Darcy remarks that she is not beautiful enough to tempt him. Elizabeth, who overhears the conversation, develops an instant dislike for Darcy.

CHAPTER 4

Jane confesses to Elizabeth how much she admires Mr. Bingley and his sisters. Elizabeth marvels at her sister's blind admiration. She can tell that while Miss Bingley and Mrs. Hurst are fine, agreeable ladies, they are proud and conceited, perhaps because they come from a respectable family in the north of England and attended one of the first private seminaries in the region. Bingley's two sisters admire and like Jane and express their desire—to Bingley and Mr. Darcy—to get to know her more.

CHAPTER 5

The morning after the assembly, the Miss Lucases visit the Miss Bennets in Longbourn to talk about the ball. The Bennets live a short walk from the property of Sir William Lucas, whose house is about a mile from Meryton. The two families are close, and the eldest of the Lucas daughters, Charlotte, is an intimate friend of Elizabeth. The ladies agree that Mr. Bingley took to Jane and that Mr. Darcy is proud and arrogant. Of his pride, Mary, who is a little empathetic, observes:

> *"Pride is a very common failing, I believe. By all that I have ever read, I am convinced that it is very common indeed; that human nature is particularly prone to it, and that there are very few of us who do not cherish a feeling of self-complacency on the score of some quality or other, real or imaginary."*

CHAPTER 6

Although Jane and Mr. Bingley have only known each other for two weeks, they have already met several times, but often in the company of others. Remarking on the couple's fondness for each other, Charlotte tells Elizabeth that it would be in Jane's best interest to drop her guard and show her affection to Bingley, lest he fails to act on his own affection for her. In defense of her sister, Elizabeth tells Charlotte that Jane is not being indifferent by design but by nature.

At a large party that Sir William Lucas assembles, Elizabeth is surprised to find Mr. Darcy listening in to her conversation with Colonel Forster. Unknown to her, Mr. Darcy—although initially cold to her—has been admiring her uncommon intelligence and playful mannerisms. Sir William Lucas asks Elizabeth to dance with Mr. Darcy, but Elizabeth firmly declines. Mr. Darcy finds himself drawn even more to her tenacity.

CHAPTER 7

Catherine and Lydia, the youngest of the Miss Bennets, visit their aunt Mrs. Phillips in Meryton and learn that a militia regiment has arrived in town and will be stationed there the whole winter. Through their aunt, the two Miss Bennets get to know some of the officers. When they get home, they talk incessantly about their admiration for the officers. Mr. Bennet, who overhears their conversation, remarks that his youngest daughters must be the silliest girls in the country.

Later on, a footman delivers a note from Miss Bingley and Mrs. Hurst. The two sisters ask for Jane's company at dinner as Mr. Bingley and his male guests are out with the officers. That evening, it rains heavily and Jane, who comes down with a cold, has to spend the night at the Bingley's.

The next morning, Elizabeth resolves to visit her sister at the Bingley's. She walks the three-mile distance between her home and Netherfield as the family's horses are committed elsewhere. By the time she gets there, her face is sweaty and her stockings are covered with dirt. When he sees her approaching the park, Mr. Darcy is torn between admiring her bravery and questioning her level-headedness. Elizabeth appreciates that Miss Bingley and Mrs. Hurst have attended well to her sister and begins to like them. She decides to stay and nurse Jane.

CHAPTER 8

After dinner, Elizabeth goes back to attend to Jane. Miss Bingley and Mrs. Hurst attack her character and disheveled appearance and remark that it was nonsensical for her to come all that way to nurse someone with a cold. The two sisters agree that with her family's low connections, Elizabeth will not find any considerable man to marry. Bingley interjects that low connections do not make the Bennets any less agreeable.

Later in the evening, Elizabeth joins Mr. Darcy, Mr. Hurst, and the Bingley's and watches them play cards. Elizabeth argues with Miss Bingley and Mrs. Hurst over what an accomplished woman should be. If an accomplished woman is one with well-rounded knowledge of music, dancing, drawing, modern languages, and gentle mannerisms, she asserts, then even the Bingley's would be hard-pressed to find such a woman.

Elizabeth goes back to Jane's room and finds that her sister's condition is getting worse. Bingley promises to call for a physician if she does not get better by morning.

CHAPTER 9

The next morning, Elizabeth sends a note to her home in Longbourn. Mrs. Bennet heeds her call and comes to visit Jane. Mrs. Bennet, who comes accompanied by her two youngest daughters, notes that Jane isn't very ill. She secretly wishes Jane doesn't recover soon as her recovery will mean she has to leave Netherfield. She reminds Mr. Bingley that Mr. Jones, the physician, recommended that Jane should not move around.

Mrs. Bennet thanks Mr. Bingley for accommodating two of her daughters and calls for her carriage to go back home. Before they leave, Lydia, the youngest of the daughters, and her mother's favorite, reminds Mr. Bingley that he promised to give a ball at Netherfield. Mr. Bingley assures her that he will, but only after Jane recovers.

CHAPTER 10

The evening of the next day, Mr. Darcy sits at a table writing a letter to his sister. Miss Bingley, who sits by his side, praises him for his meticulousness and intimates that her brother is often careless in his writing. Mr. Bingley tells his sister that his writing appears careless because his ideas flow rapidly, a remark that Mr. Darcy labels as an indirect boast. Mr. Bingley asserts that Darcy can be intolerable sometimes, especially when he is at his house on a Sunday evening.

When Mr. Darcy finishes his letter, he requests the Bingley sisters to put on some music and asks Elizabeth to dance with her. Elizabeth, who thinks he is asking to spite her, declines. Miss Bingley, who notes how much Darcy has taken to Elizabeth, feels a tinge of jealousy and contrives to get rid of Elizabeth.

CHAPTER 11

A day later, Elizabeth helps Jane—who is already feeling better—to the drawing room where the Bingley sisters welcome her. Miss Bingley's attention immediately shifts to Mr. Darcy when the gentlemen arrive. To Elizabeth's delight, Mr. Bingley sits beside Jane and engages her in conversation. Miss Bingley attempts to get Mr. Darcy's attention, but Darcy remains engrossed in the book he is reading.

Mr. Darcy only looks up when Elizabeth joins Miss Bingley—at the latter's request—in walking around the room. The trio discusses Darcy's character, who, to Elizabeth's admiration, owns his pride and temper.

CHAPTER 12

The next morning, Elizabeth writes to her mother to request a carriage to take Jane and her home. Mrs. Bennet, who is eager to have Jane stay at Netherfield a few more days, replies that the girls can't have the carriage until the following Tuesday, which will mark a week's stay at Netherfield for Jane. Elizabeth, who is eager to go home, urges Jane to borrow Mr. Bingley's carriage. Mr. Darcy is glad the Miss Bennets are leaving; the feelings he has been developing for Elizabeth are making him uncomfortable.

CHAPTER 13

The morning after Jane and Elizabeth return home, Mr. Bennet informs his wife that his cousin Mr. Collins—who has recently been ordained as a clergyman—will be visiting later in the day. Mrs. Bennet can't stand William Collins because he is to take over the Bennet estate when her husband dies. Still, she is pleased when, upon his arrival, Mr. Collins comments on the beauty of her daughters and expresses confidence that they will be married in due time.

CHAPTER 14

Over dinner, Mr. Bennet asks his cousin about his ordination. Mr. Collins takes the bait and praises Lady Catherine de Bough, his patroness, for her hospitality and kindness. He confesses that he flatters the widowed lady and her frail daughter to please them. Mr. Bennet barely hides a smug look; he has just uncovered the absurdity of his cousin.

CHAPTER 15

Mr. Collins intends to reconcile with the Bennets by offering to marry one of their daughters. He reasons that this offer is generous and in the best interest of the Bennets. Though educated, the influence of his illiterate father has made him insensible, and his position as a clergyman has filled him with equal parts pride, self-importance, and humility. He first settles for Jane but changes his mind when he discovers that she might soon be engaged. He shifts his attention to Elizabeth. Mrs. Bennet is happy with the hint, if only to get two of her daughters married.

Later in the day, Mr. Collins escorts the Bennet daughters to Meryton to visit Mrs. Phillips. At Meryton, Mary and Lydia are charmed by two officers: Mr. Denny and his friend Mr. Wickham. Mr. Wickham is handsome, has a fine figure, and addresses the ladies pleasingly. The Bennets are making easy conversations with the officers when they notice Mr. Bingley and Mr. Darcy riding their horses down the street. Elizabeth observes that Darcy avoids looking at her. She notices that when Wickham and Darcy's eyes meet, one face turns pale and the other turns red.

CHAPTER 16

The next evening, Mrs. Phillips hosts a party at her home in Meryton and invites the Miss Bennets, their cousin Mr. Collins, and the officers: Mr. Denny and Mr. Wickham. Mr. Wickham sits beside Elizabeth and the two make easy conversation. She is happy to be sitting with a man whom every woman in the room is eyeing. In the presence of the officers, the young Miss Bennets hardly take notice of Mr. Collins.

Mr. Wickham confesses to Elizabeth that although he grew up with Mr. Darcy, they have not been in good terms in a long time. Mr. Darcy's father, he expounds, was one of the best men he ever knew; generous, kind, and loving. He tells her that it hurts him to see Mr. Darcy disgrace the memory of his father. The late Mr. Darcy had been his godfather and had meant to leave him part of the Pemberley estate. However, when the senior Darcy died, his son had chosen not to honor his will. Elizabeth expresses her shock at the extent Mr. Darcy went to exert revenge on the man his father loved like his own son.

CHAPTER 17

The next day, Elizabeth relays to Jane the troubled past of Mr. Wickham and Mr. Darcy. Jane defends both men by submitting that a mistake or accident could account for what happened. Elizabeth remains adamant that Mr. Darcy is a disgraceful man and suggests that he may be imposing himself on the kinder Mr. Bingley.

Their conversation is cut short by Mr. Bingley and his sisters who visit the Bennets to invite them to a ball at Netherfield the following Tuesday. Elizabeth looks forward to dancing half the night with Mr. Wickham. When Mr. Collins asks her for the first two dances, she finds it difficult to turn him down.

CHAPTER 18

At Netherfield, Elizabeth learns, to her disappointment, that Wickham won't be attending the ball because he went to town to attend to some business. Denny implies that Wickham may be avoiding someone at the ball. Elizabeth reluctantly dances with the awkward and solemn Mr. Collins. After her second dance with Mr. Collins, Darcy takes her hand by surprise and she silently consents to dance with him. She brings up Wickham in their conversation but Darcy brushes off the subject. She questions his unappeasable resentment towards him and implies that he might be prejudiced in certain instances.

> *"It is particularly incumbent on those who never change their opinion, to be secure of judging properly at first."*

On the other side of the room, Mrs. Bennet enumerates the advantages of a union between Jane and Mr. Bingley to Lady Lucas. She conjectures that Jane's marriage to a rich man will make way for her younger sisters to marry other rich men.

CHAPTER 19

The next morning, Mr. Collins asks to speak to Elizabeth alone before he leaves for his parsonage in Hunsford. He offers to marry her, partly because her patroness insists on his marrying, and partly because he wants the estate he is to inherit from her father to remain in the family. Elizabeth thanks him for the proposal and declines it. He assures her that her refusal does not dampen his spirits; he is going to ask a second and third time because he knows she secretly wants to accept him.

CHAPTER 20

Mrs. Bennet assures Mr. Collins that she will talk to Elizabeth because, in her view, her daughter is unaware of her best interest and, consequently, foolish in rejecting his proposal. Mrs. Bennet finds her husband in the library and asks him to talk some sense to her daughter. Mr. Bennet tells Elizabeth that she is in a tight spot because she is going to become a stranger to her mother if she does not accept the proposal and a stranger to her father if she accepts it.

Mrs. Bennet tries to coerce Elizabeth to accept the proposal, but Elizabeth remains firm in her resolve not to marry Mr. Collins. She turns to Jane and then to Charlotte Lucas—who comes visiting—to help her convince Elizabeth to accept the proposal, but the two ladies refuse to interfere in the matter. The heartbroken Mrs. Bennet vows not to speak to Elizabeth again.

CHAPTER 21

The following day, Elizabeth and her sisters go to Meryton to look for Mr. Wickham. He confesses that he couldn't attend the ball because he couldn't bear being in the same room with Mr. Darcy for so long.

Back home, Jane receives a letter from Miss Bingley informing her that the party at Netherfield Park is leaving and won't get back until after winter. The Bingley sisters are going to stay in Mr. Hurst's house in Grosvenor Street as Mr. Bingley attends to business in London. Miss Bingley mentions that Mr. Bingley is eager to see Georgina Darcy and alludes to an attachment of the two. Elizabeth suspects malice in that insinuation.

CHAPTER 22

Mr. Collins, who is yet to leave Longbourn, engages Miss Lucas in conversation at dinner. Elizabeth thanks her for listening to him and abating his anger. Elizabeth is unaware that Miss Lucas has been developing some interest in Mr. Collins.

The next morning, before the Bennets realize his intentions, Mr. Collins rushes to the Lucases and meets Charlotte outside her house. He asks her to marry him, and Charlotte, who is eager to settle, accepts his proposal. Sir William and Lady Lucas consent to the union. They estimate that Mr. Collins will be a wealthy man when he inherits the Bennet estate.

Charlotte visits Elizabeth the next morning to relay the news of her engagement to Mr. Collins. The news catches Elizabeth by surprise; she can't understand how her friend would agree to marry Mr. Collins. She feels Charlotte has disgraced herself and won't be happy married to Mr. Collins.

CHAPTER 23

Mrs. Bennet can't believe that Mr. Collins is engaged to Charlotte; it has only been three days since he proposed to Elizabeth. She is convinced that Mr. Collins has been tricked and that the union can be broken off. It will be months before she forgives Elizabeth for turning down Mr. Collins.

The fact that Mr. Bingley does not write to Jane throughout winter only causes Mrs. Bennet more distress. It seems, at least to her, that none of her daughters will ever get married. She comes to develop an intense dislike for Charlotte: firstly because she is engaged to the man who should be engaged to her daughter and secondly because Charlotte will be the mistress of her house when Mr. Bennet dies.

CHAPTER 24

Miss Bingley writes to Jane to inform her that they are all settled in London for the winter. She praises Miss Darcy and mentions a growing intimacy between Mr. Darcy's sister and Mr. Bingley. Elizabeth assures Jane that Caroline's letter is part of her scheme to drive a wedge between her and Mr. Bingley. Jane, who remains despondent and unconvinced, says it's only a matter of time before she forgets Mr. Bingley.

CHAPTER 25

Towards Christmas, Mrs. Bennet receives her brother, Mr. Gardiner, and his wife, who plan to stay in Longbourn for the holidays. Mrs. Bennet expresses to Mrs. Gardiner the disappointment of having two of her daughters being so close to marriage only to lose their suitors. Mrs. Gardiner proposes to take Jane with her to her home in London to help her forget Mr. Bingley.

Over the course of several family dinners which Mr. Wickham attends, Mrs. Gardiner notices that Elizabeth and the young officer are getting very close. She resolves to warn Elizabeth about him before she leaves. She believes his account of Mr. Fitzwilliam Darcy and his son Mr. Darcy is inaccurate and self-interested.

13

Growing up, she had spent some years in Derbyshire and she remembers Mr. Fitzwilliam Darcy mentioning that Wickham was a proud and mean boy.

CHAPTER 26 3

When Mrs. Gardiner cautions Elizabeth about Mr. Wickham, Elizabeth assures her that she is not in love with him and promises to try to dissuade his interest in her.

As soon as the Gardiners leave for London with Jane, Mr. Collins returns to plan his wedding with Charlotte. The couple weds the following Thursday and leaves for Hunsford. Elizabeth, who has felt distanced from her friend since her engagement to Mr. Collins, reluctantly promises to visit Charlotte in March.

On her part, Elizabeth has managed to discourage Wickham's interest in her. She learns that he's pursuing another girl, a certain Miss King, who has inherited ten thousand pounds from her grandfather.

Jane visits Miss Bingley at the Hurst's house in Grosvenor Street when Miss Bingley fails to reply to her letter. Miss Bingley, who assures Jane that she never received her letter, informs her that Mr. Bingley and Mr. Darcy have been too busy with their business to be seen around. Jane realizes Elizabeth was right; Miss Bingley may be deceiving her.

CHAPTER 27 4

Come March, Elizabeth accompanies Sir William Lucas and his second daughter Maria to Hunsford to visit Charlotte. Elizabeth passes by the Gardiners to visit her sister and learns that Jane has had episodes of depression and has given up on being friends with Miss Bingley.

CHAPTER 28 5

The next day, Elizabeth and the Lucases travel to Hunsford to visit Mr. Collins and his wife. Mr. Collins proudly shows them around their little house and the expansive garden outside. Elizabeth is happy to find that Charlotte is content with her new life. Mrs. Jenkinson, who lives with Lady Catherine, visits with Miss de Bourgh and invites Mr. Collins and his guests to dine at the neighboring Rosings Park the following day.

CHAPTER 29 6

Mr. Collins, who leads his wife and guests to the Rosings for dinner, feels elevated by the chance to display the grandeur of his patroness. The size of the house, the innumerable attendants serving Lady Catherine, and the regal air that blankets the hall frighten Sir William and Maria Lucas, but Elizabeth remains unmoved. Elizabeth notes the sharp contrast between mother and daughter; while Lady Catherine is a tall, large, and domineering, Miss de Bough is pale, small, and embarrassingly reserved.

Lady Catherine talks extensively about her knowledge of several subjects, her benevolence, and her opinion of education and upbringing. Mr. Collins agrees to everything Lady Catherine says. At a card game, he thanks her for wining fish and apologizes when he thinks he has won too many fish.

Elizabeth contradicts Lady Cath and does answer her question about her age.

CHAPTER 30 7

Sir William stays a week at Hunsford, during which time Mr. Collins shows him around the country in his light two-wheeled carriage. Elizabeth notices that Mr. Collins goes to the Rosings every few days. She can't understand why he sacrifices so much time for his patroness. When Lady Catherine visits the Collins, she constantly examines and criticizes their furniture and routines. She deliberately looks for faults in the housemaid's work and Charlotte's cooking.

As Easter approaches, Elizabeth learns that Mr. Darcy will be visiting the Rosings in a few weeks. Lady Catherine talks about Mr. Darcy with unabated admiration.

When Mr. Darcy arrives at the Rosings, he does so in the company of Colonel Fitzwilliam, the younger son of his uncle. Colonel Fitzwilliam is about thirty and of plain looks. When Mr. Collins goes to the Rosings to pay his respects, the two men follow him back to his home. Mr. Darcy asks Elizabeth about her family, and Elizabeth asks him if he has seen Jane around town. Mr. Darcy says he hasn't, and the two men leave shortly afterwards.

CHAPTER 31 8

About a week after Mr. Darcy and Colonel Fitzwilliam arrive at the Rosings, Lady Catherine invites Charlotte and Elizabeth to her home for the evening. The party joins Lady Catherine in her drawing room for tea. Colonel Fitzwilliam, who is captivated by Elizabeth's beauty, seats beside her. The two talk with so much spirit and flow that they draw the attention of Lady Catherine and Mr. Darcy, whom the ladyship has been talking to all evening.

CHAPTER 32

Elizabeth is alone at the Collins house writing a letter to Jane when Mr. Darcy comes to visit. They talk about the possibility of Mr. Bingley never returning to Netherfield Park and the unlikely match of Mr. Collins and Charlotte. Charlotte and Maria return from their tour of the village and are surprised to find Elizabeth sitting with Darcy. Shortly afterwards, Darcy leaves. Colonel Fitzwilliam and Mr. Darcy visit the Collins fairly often afterwards, sometimes one at a time, sometimes together, and sometimes in the company of their aunt. Although Charlotte can't read the pleasant Colonel Fitzwilliam's intentions, she hopes he will marry Elizabeth.

CHAPTER 33

By pure chance, Elizabeth meets Mr. Darcy as she takes a solitary walk around Rosing Park. Mr. Darcy offers to escort Elizabeth back and surprises her when he asks if she will be staying for long when she visits the Collins again.

On another walk, Colonel Fitzwilliam escorts her back to the parsonage. He informs her that he is leaving Kent on Saturday with Mr. Darcy, if he does not change his mind again. Of Darcy's caprice, he notes:

> "He likes to have his own way very well... But so we all do. It is only that he has better means of having it than many others, because he is rich, and many others are poor."

When Elizabeth brings up the subject of the peculiar relationship between Darcy and Bingley, Colonel Fitzwilliam tells Elizabeth that Mr. Bingley may be indebted to Mr. Darcy. He tells her that Mr. Darcy once mentioned to him that he saved a friend from an imprudent marriage. Colonel Fitzwilliam suspects that the friend Darcy alluded to is Mr. Bingley. Elizabeth begins to understand that Darcy may be the cause of Jane's misery.

CHAPTER 34

Elizabeth reviews the letters Jane has written to her since she came to Kent and realizes that her sister's characteristic cheerfulness has faded. She is alone poring over the letters when the doorbell rings and Mr. Darcy walks in. He takes Elizabeth by utter surprise when he professes his love for her. He confesses that he has tried in vain to suppress his feelings for her and asks her to marry him. Elizabeth tells him that she is unaware of any feelings of affection towards her and declines the proposal. She adds that she could never think well of a man who ruined her sister's happiness, and that she knew he was the last man on earth she would want to marry the day she met him.

Mr. Darcy admits, rather shamelessly, and with a hint of pride, that he did everything in his power to separate Jane and Bingley. He tells Elizabeth that while his feelings for her were natural and just, he found it hard to admit to himself that he could love a woman whose condition in life was far below his own.

CHAPTER 35

The next morning, Elizabeth takes a walk near the park to calm her mind. Mr. Darcy, who has been walking in the park, catches up with her and gives her a letter. He asks her to read it and walks away. In the letter, Mr. Darcy tells Elizabeth that while Mr. Bingley was in love with Jane, Darcy could tell that Jane was only indifferent towards Bingley. He adds that he was sure Mr. Bingley and Jane could not get along well because Jane and her sisters, with the exception of Elizabeth, were too eager to censure themselves and conform to the standards of their hosts at Netherfield Park.

As to his dispute with Mr. Wickham, Mr. Darcy informs Elizabeth that when his father died, he left Mr. Wickham a thousand pounds and recommended that he get a share of his estate if he became a clergyman. Since Mr. Wickham did not want to be a clergyman, Mr. Darcy gave him three thousand pounds to pay for his law studies. Three years later, Mr. Wickham—who never went to study law but idled around and wasted the money—wrote to Mr. Darcy informing him that he had resolved to become a clergyman and wanted his share of the estate. When, in good judgment, Mr. Darcy refused to grant his request, Mr. Wickham developed an intense hatred for him. A few months later, Mr. Wickham had attempted to elope with the then fifteen-year-old Georgiana Darcy to get a share of her fortune and exert his revenge, but Mr. Darcy had caught up with him and thwarted his scheme.

CHAPTER 36

While the bold contention that Mr. Darcy had the right to interfere in Jane and Bingley's affairs angers Elizabeth, she realizes that the accusations Mr. Wickham made against him were all false. She recalls that while Mr. Darcy was still at Netherfield Park, Mr. Wickham told no one but her the injustices that Mr. Darcy

17

committed. Only after Mr. Darcy left Netherfield did Mr. Wickham make the injustices publicly known—even though he had assured her that he had too much respect for Mr. Darcy's father to expose his son. She realizes this scheme was a cowardly act, as was refusing to attend the ball at Netherfield Park. Of this realization, she remarks:

> "How despicably I have acted! I, who have prided myself on my discernment! I, who have valued myself on my abilities! ... Pleased with the preference of one, and offended by the neglect of the other, on the very beginning of our acquaintance, I have courted prepossession and ignorance, and driven reason away, where either were concerned. Till this moment I never knew myself."

CHAPTER 37

Mr. Darcy and Colonel Fitzwilliam leave the Rosings the next morning. Lady Catherine, who is already feeling dull, invites Mr. Collins and his guests for dinner. She persuades Elizabeth to stay at the parsonage a little longer, but Elizabeth insists that she has to leave the following Saturday.

CHAPTER 38

On Saturday—having stayed at the parsonage for six weeks—Elizabeth and Maria Lucas leave Hunsford. Mr. Collins thanks them for their visit and asks Elizabeth to relay home, as she has witnessed, that Charlotte is happy at the parsonage and well-liked by the Rosings. The carriage drops Elizabeth and Maria at Mr. Gardiner's house where the two are to stay for a few days and leave for Longbourn with Jane.

CHAPTER 39

The second week of May, Elizabeth, Jane, and Maria leave Gracechurch Street and head to Hertfordshire. They find Kitty and Lydia in a in town inn watching the sentinel on guard. Lydia informs them that the soldiers are leaving Meryton to camp near Brighton for the summer. She intends to ask her father to take the family there for the summer.

Back home, when Lydia suggests that the girls should walk to Meryton, Elizabeth opposes the plan. She intends to avoid Mr. Wickham as much as she can.

CHAPTER 40

The next morning, Elizabeth narrates to Jane what happened between her and Mr. Darcy. Jane agrees that he was mistaken to think Elizabeth would accept his proposal but empathizes with the pain he had to endure when Elizabeth disappointed him. Elizabeth admits that she was wrong to judge him so harshly. She tells Jane that she does not intend to expose Mr. Wickham as he will be gone soon, and she does not intend to exonerate Mr. Darcy as the people of Meryton are too prejudiced to change their opinion of him.

Elizabeth observes that Jane is still in love with Mr. Bingley. She intentionally leaves out what Mr. Darcy admitted about breaking them up in the hope that Bingley will tell Jane why he never kept in touch when they meet again.

CHAPTER 41

The second week after Jane and Elizabeth get home, the regiment at Meryton prepares to leave for Brighton. Lydia and Kitty are heartbroken; their father won't take them to Brighton. When Mrs. Forster, the wife of the colonel of the regiment and a friend to Lydia, invites Lydia to accompany her to Brighton, Lydia is overjoyed. Elizabeth asks her father not to let Lydia go to Brighton lest her flirtatious behavior becomes unmanageable and brings shame to the family. Mr. Bennet tells Elizabeth that Lydia needs to go to learn her own insignificance and realize the futility of her pursuits.

On the last day of the regiment's stay in Meryton, some of the officers go to dine at Longbourn. Elizabeth mentions to an alarmed Mr. Wickham that, for three weeks, she was almost always in the company of Mr. Darcy and Colonel Fitzwilliam at Hunsford. She adds that her opinion of him has improved after she got to know him better. Mr. Wickham tries to talk about the injustice Mr. Darcy did him, but Elizabeth refuses to engage him on the subject. At the end of the evening, neither Elizabeth nor Wickham has any desire to see the other again.

CHAPTER 42

Three weeks after Lydia leaves for Brighton with Mrs. Forster, Longbourn begins to regain its usual cheerfulness. Elizabeth reflects on her negative assessment of marriage; the impression her parent's relationship has given her has not been very favorable. Still, she is happy that Kitty is getting over being left behind by Lydia.

Later in the summer, the Gardiners visit Longbourn, leave their four children under the care of Jane, and head off to tour the country with Elizabeth. They travel through Oxford, Birmingham, some other little-known towns, and settle in Derbyshire. When Mrs. Gardiner suggests they visit Pemberley, Elizabeth is distressed by the thought of running into Mr. Darcy. A maid puts her at ease when she divulges that the family is away for the summer.

CHAPTER 43

The next morning, Gardiners drive by Pemberley with Elizabeth. She marvels at the vastness of the park and the beauty of the large Pemberley house. As the Gardiners express their admiration of the park, it crosses Elizabeth's mind that it would mean something to be the mistress of Pemberley.

The trio walks to the house and the housekeeper welcomes them in. Elizabeth realizes that the rooms, with all their splendor, could have been hers had she accepted Mr. Darcy's proposal. She banishes the thought before it morphs into regret. The housekeeper informs them that the owner will be back the following day with some friends. She praises Miss Darcy's beauty and accomplishments and adds that she has never heard an unkind word from Mr. Darcy.

Elizabeth wonders how her opinion of Mr. Darcy could be so different from that of the housekeeper and longs to hear more about him. The housekeeper goes on and talks about him being the best master she has ever met; he is friendly to the poor, considerate about other people's needs, and committed to doing anything for his sister. She adds that people only think he is proud because he does not talk as much as other young men.

Elizabeth and the Gardiners leave the house and walk towards the garden. Suddenly, Mr. Darcy appears from the road behind the stables. He is as surprised to see Elizabeth as she is to see him. They talk for a few minutes, but the conversation becomes uncomfortable and he leaves. Elizabeth feels ashamed that Mr. Darcy found her at his house; he must think she is throwing herself at him.

They leave the compound and walk by the river in the woods, where they run into Mr. Darcy again. Elizabeth introduces the Gardiners to Mr. Darcy, who is surprised to learn that they are her relatives. She is proud to show him that she has relatives she does not feel ashamed of. Mr. Darcy invites Mr. Gardiner to fish at the river whenever he likes.

As she walks alongside Darcy, Elizabeth assures him that she did not know he would be around. Darcy admits he came back earlier than he had planned and informs her that his sister would like to meet her. They walk the rest of the distance to the carriage in awkward silence. On their way from Pemberley, the Gardiners find it difficult to understand how Elizabeth could have described Mr. Darcy as disagreeable.

CHAPTER 44

The next day, Mr. Darcy and his sister visit the inn where Elizabeth is staying and ask to see her. The Gardiners realize that, with all the effort he is making, Mr. Darcy must be in love with Elizabeth. Elizabeth is surprised to find that Miss Darcy is not the proud girl that people make her to be. On the contrary, she is exceedingly shy. While she is only sixteen, she is taller than Elizabeth, womanly, and gentle.

A few moments after Mr. Darcy introduces his sister, Mr. Bingley enters the room and joins them. He asks about her family, and Elizabeth realizes that her resentment towards him is long gone. She observes Bingley's interaction with Miss Darcy and is content to find that they are not nearly as close as Miss Bingley implied. When Bingley accurately recalls the last time he danced with Jane, she conjectures that he might still have feelings for her.

Elizabeth notices that Mr. Darcy is friendly to people he would not have talked to in the past and realizes that something in him has permanently changed; he is eager to please, polite, and unreserved. When they leave, Mr. Darcy invites Elizabeth and her uncle and aunt to dinner at Permberley before they leave the country. When the party leaves, Elizabeth feels ashamed for disliking him so intensely only a few months ago. The shame gives way to gratitude as she considers that he still loves her, even after rejecting him and making false accusations against him.

CHAPTER 45

The following morning, Mr. Gardiner goes fishing and Mrs. Gardiner and Elizabeth return Miss Darcy's visit. At Pemberley, they are received by Miss Bingley, Mrs. Hurst, and Miss Georgiana Darcy. Elizabeth realizes that Miss Bingley is closely watching her. She can't tell whether she wishes for or fears Mr. Darcy will join them.

Mr. Darcy, who leaves his friends fishing to entertain his guests, joins the ladies soon afterwards. Miss Bingley coerces Elizabeth to talk about the soldiers who were stationed at Meryton in the hope that she will give away her fondness for Mr. Wickham. Elizabeth evades the subject. When she leaves shortly afterwards, Miss

Bingley criticizes her personality and appearance, but Georgiana, to whom the effusions are directed, refuses to join in the criticism. To Miss Bingley's vexation, Mr. Darcy admits that while he never found Elizabeth beautiful when they first met, he can't help but think that she is one of the most beautiful women he knows.

CHAPTER 46

A few days later, Elizabeth receives two letters from Jane. She learns from her sister, as Jane learned from Colonel Forster, that Lydia has ran off to Scotland with one of the officers: Mr. Wickham. Jane comforts Elizabeth by adding that Mr. Wickham's intentions must be sincere as he knows that their father has nothing for Lydia to inherit.

In the second letter, dated a day after the first, Jane tells Elizabeth that Lydia and Wickham did not go to Scotland as planned. She narrates that colonel Forster, upon finding out that Wickham never intended to go to Scotland or marry Lydia, went after them but lost their trace at Clapham. Mr. Bennet intends to accompany Colonel Forster to London to look for her. She adds that although her mother and father are disturbed by the news, she is optimistic it will turn out well.

Elizabeth meets Mr. Darcy at the door of the inn as he rushes to look for Mr. and Mrs. Gardiner and share the news. Mr. Darcy sends his servant to look for the Gardiners and calms the visibly shaken Elizabeth. She recounts what happened and blames herself for not doing anything with her knowledge of Wickham to prevent the elopement.

CHAPTER 47

On the carriage travelling to Longbourn, the Gardiners assure Elizabeth that Mr. Wickham would not risk his military career to elope with a friendless and fortuneless girl unless it was for something else. Elizabeth wonders what, beyond Lydia's youth, health, and good humor, Wickham could want from her. Had she known Lydia was fond of Wickham, she would have warned her about him when she left for Brighton.

About a day and half later, Elizabeth and the Gardiners arrive in Longbourn. Elizabeth learns from Jane that their father has already left for town to look for Lydia. Mrs. Bennet curses Wickham for his wicked act and for causing her suffering. She blames the Forsters for neglecting her daughter. It does not occur to her that Lydia's impulsive choices may be a consequence of a lenient and misguided upbringing.

CHAPTER 48

In Meryton, Wickham, who was the perfect model of a gentleman only three months ago, quickly gains a reputation as the wickedest man on earth. It emerges that he has business and gaming debts of a considerable amount in both Brighton and Meryton.

On Sunday, Mr. Gardiner leaves for London, finds Mr. Bennet, and persuades him to go back home to ease his wife's anxiety. Mr. Bennet insists on checking all the main hotels in town, and Mr. Gardiner reluctantly agrees. Mr. Gardiner writes to Colonel Forster and asks him to enquire from the officers if Wickham has any relations in town he might visit. Mr. Forster informs him that Wickham was not particularly close to any of the other officers.

Mr. Collins writes to Mr. Bennet to remark on the shame Lydia has brought on his family. He implies that it would have been better if she had died.

Mr. Bennet returns home and confesses to Elizabeth that he is to blame for not heeding her advice to stop Lydia from going to Brighton. He resolves to be stricter with Kitty.

CHAPTER 49

Two days later, Mr. Bennet receives a letter from Mr. Gardiner. Mr. Gardiner informs him that he has found Wickham and Lydia, and that he has taken Lydia to his home. The two, he adds, are not yet married. They have asked that Mr. Bennet to promise to give Lydia an allowance of one hundred pounds a year and an inheritance of five thousand pounds upon his death before they proceed with the engagement. Mr. Gardiner promises that Wickham's debts will be repaid.

While Mr. Bennet is troubled by the thought that he may not be able to repay Mr. Gardiner, Mrs. Bennet is overjoyed to find that there is a chance Wickham and Lydia will soon be married. Jane reminds her mother that Mr. Gardiner has had to settle Mr. Wickham's debts. Mrs. Bennet comments that it is Mr. Gardiner's responsibility to provide for his niece.

CHAPTER 50

Mr. Bennet, who is surprised that Wickham did not ask for much, agrees to the couple's demands and instructs Mr. Gardiner to proceed with his plans to formalize the union. Mrs. Bennet busies herself with plans about what Lydia will wear on her wedding and what house the newly-wed couple will settle into in Longbourn. Mr. Bennet informs her that he will not encourage their impertinence; he will see to it that they don't settle anywhere near Longbourn. He refuses, to his wife's horror, to give any money for the purchase of Lydia's clothes.

Elizabeth wonders whether Mr. Darcy would want anything to do with a family whose daughter is married to a man he vehemently hates. It is only now, when the chances of a relationship between them are lowest, that she realizes she could have been happy with him.

Mr. Gardiner writes to Mr. Bennet to inform him that Wickham is quitting the army and joining a regular regiment in the north, where she will be living with Lydia. He adds that he has compiled a list of his creditors and intends to settle the debts in a week. He asks if Lydia can see her family before she leaves for the north and Mr. Bennet reluctantly agrees.

CHAPTER 51

The day of the wedding, Lydia and her fiancée travel to Longbourn to the reception of a cold father, an overjoyed mother, and anxious sisters. Lydia is her usual wild and noisy self, and Wickham exerts a calm and reassuring character. Lydia, who is in high spirits, boasts that she has taken Jane's place as a married woman and declares that she will get husbands for her sisters when they visit her in Newcastle.

Elizabeth notes that Wickham does not care for Lydia as much as Lydia cares for him. She conjectures that they eloped because Lydia pushed him to it. Lydia recounts to Elizabeth how she got married at St. Clement's in the company of an unpleasant Mr. and Mrs. Gardiner. She mentions that Mr. Darcy was at her wedding ~~and implies that she could have married him had Wickham not showed up.~~ Elizabeth, who is incredibly curious, writes to Mrs. Gardiner to ask what business Mr. Darcy had at her sister's wedding.

CHAPTER 52   10

Elizabeth learns from Mrs. Gardiner that Mr. Darcy left Derbyshire to look for Wickham and Lydia because he felt their elopement was a wrong he needed to right. He found the two after bribing Mrs. Younge—who had once been the governess of Miss Darcy and who had arranged for her elopement with Mr. Wickham – to disclose their whereabouts. Mr. Darcy attempted to convince Lydia to return home but her only desire was to be with Wickham. Seeing that she had already resolved to stay, he talked to Wickham about expediting their marriage. Mr. Darcy realized that Wickham had never intended to marry Lydia; he had been making plans to leave the regiment on account of his debts when the plan to elope came to mind.

Mrs. Gardiner adds that it was Mr. Darcy who, after agreeing to meet Wickham's demands, convinced him to get married to Lydia. He waited until Mr. Bennet left London to inform Mr. Gardiner what he had discovered and what he was planning. Mr. Gardiner wanted to settle Wickham's debts, but Mr. Darcy insisted on settling the debts and letting Mr. Gardiner take the credit. After settling Wickham's debts, Mr. Darcy went to Pemberley and returned to attend the wedding.

Elizabeth wonders how Mr. Darcy could have gone to all that trouble for a man he disliked so much and for a girl who could hardly afford his respect.

CHAPTER 53   11

Mrs. Bennet is sulking over the departure of Wickham and Lydia when she receives news that the housekeeper of Netherfield Park is preparing for the arrival of her master who is to stay there for several weeks. She pretends not to care about the news, but she is secretly happy about the prospect it brings. Jane tries to assure Elizabeth that despite her distressed appearance, she is not moved by the news. Elizabeth is not convinced that Jane would regard Mr. Bingley with indifference.

Mrs. Bennet tries to persuade her husband to go see Mr. Bingley when he comes—like he had done a year before—but Mr. Bennet remains adamant that such a visit would be a fool's errand.

A few days after their arrival at Netherfield Park, Mr. Bingley and Mr. Darcy visit the Bennets. Mrs. Bennet sees the two men approaching and expresses her dislike for Mr. Darcy. She mentions that he is only welcome at her home because he is Bingley's friend. Elizabeth is still the only one who knows the role Darcy played in getting Lydia married.

Mrs. Bennet talks to Mr. Bingley about his stay at Netherfield and Lydia's wedding. Elizabeth remains silent at the table and hardly looks at Mr. Darcy. She realizes that Jane, who hardly talked to Bingley when he came in, is giving him more attention. When the gentlemen rise to leave, Mrs. Bennet arranges to have them over for dinner in a few days' time.

CHAPTER 54   12

Elizabeth paces around the lawn trying to understand why Mr. Darcy would come to visit and remain silent and indifferent. She resolves not to think about him anymore.

On Tuesday, Mr. Bingley and Mr. Darcy join about a dozen guests at the Bennets for dinner. Mrs. Bennet has Jane sit by herself, and Mr. Bingley has no option but to sit beside her. After dinner, the guests head to the drawing room to take tea and play card games. Elizabeth hopes Mr. Darcy will sit beside her, but another girl takes the place she has reserved for him. Mrs. Bennet notes Mr. Bingley's attitude towards Jane and convinces herself that they will end up together.

CHAPTER 55   13

A few days after the dinner, Mrs. Bennet invites Mr. Bingley to dine at her home again. Mr. Bingley notifies the Bennets that Mr. Darcy is in London for business and won't be back until after ten days. Mrs. Bennet rushes Jane, who is still dressing, to go downstairs to meet Mr. Bingley, but Jane refuses to go without the company of at least one of her sisters.

After tea, Mr. Bennet leaves for his library and Mary goes upstairs to play her instruments. Mrs. Bennet winks at Elizabeth and Kitty in the hope that they will leave the room to Jane and Mr. Bingley, but neither Elizabeth nor Kitty reads her intentions. Mr. Bingley is cheerful throughout his visit, and Elizabeth observes that Jane has lost her indifference towards him.

The next day Mr. Bingley visits again and goes to shoot birds with Mr. Bennet. After dinner, Mrs. Bennet manages to get Mr. Bingley and Jane alone in the drawing room. When Elizabeth walks into the drawing room, she is surprised to find Bingley and Jane standing close together near the fireplace.

When Jane emerges from the drawing room, she relates to her family that her relationship with Mr. Bingley is settled. When she hears the news, the overjoyed

Mrs. Bennet praises Mr. Bingley for half an hour. Even Mr. Bennet can't hide the happiness in his voice and manners.

From then on, Bingley becomes a daily visitor at Longbourn. He confesses to Jane that he still loved her when he went away in November. The only reason he never came back sooner was because he was convinced she was indifferent towards him. The news of their engagement spread throughout Meryton and, consequently, the town comes into agreement that the Bennets must be luckiest family in the world.

CHAPTER 56

About a week after the engagement, the Bennets are sitting in the dining room when a chaise drives up the lawn and Lady Catherine de Bough walks in. She sits without saying a word, and Elizabeth makes some hurried introductions.

Lady Catherine asks Elizabeth to take a walk with her on the lawn. She tells Elizabeth that she has heard that Jane is engaged to Bingley and that Elizabeth may soon be engaged to her nephew, Mr. Darcy. She asks, quite contemptuously, whether Mr. Darcy has proposed to her. When Elizabeth evades her questions, Lady Catherine conjectures that she must be drawing Mr. Darcy in.

She tells Elizabeth that Mr. Darcy's engagement to Miss de Bough was planned since the two were infants and adds that she is determined to see to it that a woman without family, connections, or fortune will not foil her plans. Elizabeth tells Lady Catherine that her plans for her daughter will not prevent her from accepting Darcy's proposal, if he asks. When Lady Catherine warns her that everyone connected to Mr. Darcy will censure and disregard her if she marries him, Elizabeth observes that she will have a lot of other things to keep her happy.

She tries, fruitlessly, to make Elizabeth promise that she won't enter into an engagement with Mr. Darcy. She cites the dishonor it would bring Mr. Darcy to marry into her family, but Elizabeth remains resolute that she will act in the interest of her happiness, however much it inconveniences others. Lady Catherine makes more threats and leaves.

CHAPTER 57

The next morning, Mr. Bennet calls Elizabeth to his library and informs her that he has received a letter from Mr. Collins. In the letter, Mr. Collins surmises that a certain gentleman is about to propose to her and warns that the proposal may come with its fair share of evils as Lady Catherine does not approve of it. Mr. Bennet is pleasantly surprised that Mr. Darcy—whom he knows has a reputation of finding faults in women—would want to marry Elizabeth.

CHAPTER 58

A few days after Lady Catherine's visit, Mr. Bingley visits the Bennets and brings Mr. Darcy with him. At Mr. Bingley's suggestion, the Bennet daughters talk a walk with the gentlemen, Jane with Bingley, and Elizabeth, Mary, and Kitty with Darcy.

When Elizabeth is alone with Darcy, she thanks him for everything he did for Lydia. Darcy tells her that he was thinking only of her when he was helping Lydia. He asks if her sentiments towards him have changed since he proposed, and Elizabeth confesses, to the delight of Darcy, that they have significantly changed. She mentions that his letter had abated her prejudice. Darcy admits that as an only son, he was spoilt by his parents and taught to think of no one outside his family. He confesses to Elizabeth that he would still have been that person had it not been for her.

Darcy tells Elizabeth that before he left for London, he confessed to a surprised Bingley how he interfered with his relationship with Jane. He told him that he purposely kept her visit in London secret and admitted that he was wrong to think Jane was indifferent to him. He tells Elizabeth that he knew, following his confession, that Bingley would propose soon afterwards.

CHAPTER 59

When Elizabeth gets back home, she decides to tell Jane that she is engaged to Mr. Darcy. She knows that no one in her family, except Jane, likes him and wonders how her parents and sisters will get over their dislike for him. The news catches Jane by surprise; she always thought Elizabeth hated Mr. Darcy.

The next morning, Mrs. Bennet is looking out of the window of her house when she sees Mr. Bingley and Mr. Darcy approaching. She wonders when Darcy will grow tired of visiting her home and stop upsetting everyone. She suggests that Elizabeth and Kitty walk with Darcy outside to get him out of Bingley's way. When Kitty excuses herself, Mrs. Bennet apologizes to Elizabeth for making her put up with the company of a disagreeable man. As Elizabeth walks with Mr. Darcy towards the mountains, she wonders how her mother will take the news of her engagement to Darcy. She suspects that his wealth will do little to lessen the hatred she has reserved for him.

In the evening, Mr. Darcy follows Mr. Bennet to his library and informs him of his intention to marry Elizabeth. Mr. Bennet calls Elizabeth to his library and, when they are alone, asks her if it is not true that she always hated Darcy. He is convinced that, against her better judgment, she is marrying him for his wealth. She wishes she hadn't judged him so harshly before; it would have been easier to explain to her family her change of heart.

Elizabeth relates to her father what Darcy did for Lydia and how he has changed in the months that she has known him. She manages to convince him that Darcy is the right match for her, and Mr. Bennet wishes her happiness in her marriage.

When she leaves the library, Elizabeth follows her mother to her dressing room and relays the news to her. Mrs. Bennet remains silent for some time and, when she finally speaks, exclaims how rich Elizabeth will be when she marries Darcy. She remarks that Mr. Darcy is tall and handsome and apologizes for disliking him. For Mrs. Bennet, the fact that her daughter is getting married to a man who earns ten thousand pounds a year makes up for everything she hated about him.

CHAPTER 60

Elizabeth coerces Mr. Darcy to admit that he fell in love with her because she was different from the other women he knew. She wonders how long he would have taken—all those times he came to dine at Longbourn—to talk to her had she not encouraged it. He confesses that, ironically, it was Lady Catherine's attempts to separate them that convinced him of her resolve to be with him.

Darcy goes to write to Lady Catherine to give her news of his engagement, and Elizabeth goes to write to the Gardiners. Lady Catherine is so angered by the news that Mr. Collins and Charlotte, who is thrilled to hear her friend is getting married, have to leave for Longbourn until her rage dissipates.

CHAPTER 61

The day Jane and Elizabeth get married is the day an ecstatic Mrs. Bennet feels accomplished as a mother.

Mr. Bennet misses Elizabeth the most and often makes unannounced visits at Pemberley. Mr. Bingley and Jane stay at Netherfield for a year before moving to Derbyshire, where Mr. Bingley bought an estate about thirty miles away from Pemberley. Kitty spends most of her time with Jane or Elizabeth. Thanks to the influence of high society, she is becoming more agreeable and ladylike. Her father has forbidden her from visiting Lydia despite her sister's numerous invitations. Mary remains at home with her parents. She is content that she does not have to compare herself to them anymore.

Lydia is happy her eldest sisters are now married. She has written to Elizabeth to ask her to consider asking Mr. Darcy to give her family some yearly allowance in lieu of Wickham's inheritance, but Elizabeth is not open to the suggestion; she has already heard of the Wickhams' extravagance. Darcy still can't bear to have Wickham at Pemberley but he assists him—for Elizabeth's sake—advance in his profession.

Elizabeth and Georgiana, who still stays at Pemberley, are getting closer by the day.

When Lady Catherine replies to Mr. Darcy's letter, she expresses her anger over what she thinks is an unsuitable marriage and mocks Elizabeth. In time, Elizabeth persuades Darcy to reach out to his aunt and make peace with her.

ABOUT THE AUTHOR

Jane Austen was a British novelist whose works transcended cultural boundaries to make her one of the most renowned romance writers of all time. Her six novels, whose plots touch on the excesses of 18th century British social classes and the dependence of women on marriage, achieved print success and inspired scores of writers who have experimented with her style.

Born in rural Steventon, Hampshire, in 1775, Jane grew up with a sister, a brother, and parents who openly discussed contentious political and social subjects. This easy intellectual atmosphere and her sister's tales of London may have shaped the social commentary evident in Jane's novels. She attended school at Oxford but was later home educated when she caught typhus and almost died. From when she was eleven, Jane wrote poems and short stories to amuse herself and her family.

When she was about twenty, Jane was attracted to Tom Lefroy, a neighbor who had just completed his university degree. However, their relationship was impractical as neither Jane nor Tom had any money. The Lefroy family sent Tom away and kept him from the Austens whenever he visited Hampshire. Her brief and abortive relationship with Tom may have inspired the characters of her fictional namesake, Jane, and the tortuous relationship she shares with Bingley in *Pride and Prejudice*.

In 1809, Jane's brother moved the family to a large and quiet cottage in Chawton village where she published four of her novels. *Pride and Prejudice*, which was published in 1813, became an immediate success. Her most successful novel, at least financially, was *Mansfield Park*. She never got the fame she is accorded today because she published her novels anonymously.

Jane died from Addison's disease in 1817, at the age of 41.

MAJOR CHARACTERS

Elizabeth Bennet

The second daughter of the Bennet family and the protagonist of *Pride and Prejudice*, Elizabeth is intelligent, observant, and bold. Keen and judgmental, she prides herself on being a good reader of situations and character but realizes there are limits to her intuition.

Jane Bennet

The eldest of the Bennet daughters, Jane is optimistic, kind, assumes the best in others, and never speaks ill of anyone. Her innocence borders naivety; she is unaware of her beauty and thinks there isn't as much scheming in the world as people imagine. Her calm and reserved demeanor is interpreted as indifference, and she almost loses Bingley for it.

Fitzwilliam Darcy

The only son in a wealthy, respected family and the master of the expansive Pemberley estate, Darcy is the most misunderstood character in the novel. The tall and handsome man comes off as proud, disagreeable, and harsh but develops an unusual humility and eagerness to please when Elizabeth rejects him.

Charles Bingley

Unlike his best friend Mr. Darcy, Bingley is friendly, good-natured, and accommodating of people outside his social class. The object of Jane's affection, Bingley comes off as a diffident man who desperately relies on his best friend's opinions and judgment.

Mr. Bennet

The patriarch of the Bennet household, Mr. Bennet, although reasonable, comes off as indolent, aloof, and unconcerned with his family's affairs. Married to Mrs. Bennet for twenty-three years, he finds his wife ridiculous and refuses to give in to her self-interested requests. The library is his escape from his family's drama, and he uses sarcastic humor to mask his feelings.

Mrs. Bennet

The wife of Mr. Bennet, Mrs. Bennet is ignorant, discontent with her social status, and solely concerns herself with getting her five daughters married. A self-absorbed woman, she considers other people's words and actions to be personal attacks. She is peevish, capricious, and complains a lot, her justification being that "Those who do not complain are never pitied."

Charlotte Lucas

The eldest of the Sir William Lucas daughters, Charlotte is Elizabeth's best friend. At twenty-seven, Charlotte is a self-confessed unromantic; she doesn't care much about who she gets married to, as long as she gets married.

Mr. William Collins

Cousin to Mr. Bennet and later on, husband to Charlotte Lucas, Mr. Collins is always eager to please wealthy patrons. He comes off as unreasonable and absurd; he thinks it better for Lydia to die than elope with Wickham. He also comes off as self-deceptive; he takes Elizabeth's refusal to marry him as encouragement to ask a second and third time.

Miss Caroline Bingley

Sister to Mr. Bingley and Mrs. Hurst, Caroline is cunning, calculating, and unaccommodating of don't fit into her social class or her devious plans. She makes passes at Mr. Darcy and contrives to get rid of Elizabeth and her sister when she discovers that the object of her affection is captivated by Elizabeth.

George Wickham

One of the officers who catch Lydia and Kitty's attention. An embittered social climber and extravagant, Wickham hides his true nature behind pleasing expressions and charming mannerisms.

Lydia and Kitty Bennet

The youngest of the Bennet daughters, Lydia and Kitty spend most of their time together observing and pursuing military officers. They come off as untamed, indulgent, and carefree. Lydia, who is only sixteen, becomes the source of her family's agony when she elopes with Wickham.

Mary Bennet

The least notable of the Bennet daughters, Mary compensates for her plain looks by accumulating knowledge and accomplishments, of which she is always eager to show off.

THEMES

Love and marriage

Elizabeth thinks marriage is only justified if it is based on love. Charlotte thinks marriage should guarantee security and a material life, and that love in marriage is only a matter of luck. These contrasting views represent the opinions of the other characters. Mrs. Bennet would prefer to have her daughters married to wealthy men, but she will take anyone, including a debtor, for a son-in-law.

Family

The Bennet family is a model of dissimilarity and incongruence, as is always the case with any social unit. The reader meets a satirical and aloof father, an unreasonable mother, a kind and naïve first-born daughter, a keen and bold second-born, two flirtatious and ignorant sisters, and an insecure sister.

Society and class

The sharp contrast between the middle-class Bennet family and the upper-class Bingley and Darcy families makes relationships between the two families difficult to navigate. Social gatherings are opportunities for making comparisons and belittling those with lesser means. As Mr. Bennet notes:

> *"For what do we live, but to make sport for our neighbors, and laugh at them in our turn?"*

Wealth

Wealth plays a big role in determining who interacts with whom and who marries whom. Mrs. Bennet is keen to have her daughters marry wealthy men. For women, marrying well is the only guarantee of a good life. Even Wickham is looking to marry a wealthy woman. The restriction of inheritance to male heirs is a source of significant grievance for the Bennets who have no son.

Pride

Almost every character prides him/herself of some aspect. Darcy is too proud to dance or converse with the simple people of Meryton. Even Elizabeth prides herself in her ability to read and understand character.

Prejudice

Darcy thinks the middle-class inhabitants of Meryton are dull until Elizabeth captivates him with her unusual intelligence and wit. Elizabeth thinks wealthy people are arrogant and calculating until she finds Darcy's softer side.

Women and femininity

Miss Bingley's idea of an accomplished woman is one who can sing and dance, one who knows multiple languages, and one who has praiseworthy mannerisms. Mary believes that when a woman loses her virtue, she can never regain it. Evidently, the same cannot be said of the men in the novel.

Deceit

Mr. Wickham, the model of deceit in the novel, uses charm and pretense to get Elizabeth to his side, to try and get a share of the Pemberley estate, and to have others settle his debts. Miss Bingley contrives devious schemes, with the help of Darcy, to separate Bingley and Jane.

ANALYSIS

In *Pride and Prejudice*, the narrator assumes a superior knowledge of the characters from the beginning. The nature of the characters is revealed more by the narrator than by their actions, conversations, or thoughts. She informs the reader that Bingley will become the property of someone's daughter even before he does and divulges that Mrs. Bennet is ignorant and capricious before the reader ascertains the fact. Although the book follows the life of Elizabeth and her sisters, the protagonist is not the reader's constant companion or primary friend; the narrator has comfortably assumed that role.

No more evident is the narrator's superior claim to the character's dispositions than in the title. She labels the book "pride and prejudice" as opposed to "Elizabeth and Darcy" or "a tale of love and class" to give the reader the hint that she already knows who is proud and who is prejudiced. It is the suspense—the eagerness to determine for oneself who is arrogant and who harbors baseless preconceptions—that draws the reader in. In a sense, by alluding to some sort of superior knowledge, the narrator forces the reader to trust her judgment.

All the same, the narrator is subtle in her hints about what comes next, how the characters change, and how the story progresses beyond the ending. It may seem as if the story ends like a neatly packed fairytale—where everyone gets married and lives happily ever after—but the narrator hints at a lot of progress in those last few pages. For one, Elizabeth, Jane, Bingley and Darcy have managed to break off the class shackles of their time and, against all odds and contrary to popular advice, married for love. What's more, the narrator hints that these marriages are only the first in a wave of social change where people of other classes become more acceptable to first-class folks. Despite initially dismissing Elizabeth as a low-life, for example, Lady Catherine de Bough comes around and expresses a desire to get to know her. Miss Bingley may have the same change of heart with Jane and even marry someone from a lower social class, who knows?

END

If you enjoyed this summary and analysis, please leave an honest review on Amazon.com.

If you haven't already, we encourage you to purchase a copy of the original book!

Made in the USA
Columbia, SC
19 November 2020